Date: 10/11/13

Woodpecker

by Dee Phillips

Consultants:

Kevin J. McGowan, PhD
Cornell Lab of Ornithology, Ithaca, New York

Kimberly Brenneman, PhD
National Institute for Early Education Research, Rutgers University, New Brunswick, New Jersey

New York, New York

Credits

Cover, © iStockphoto/Thinkstock; 2–3, © Deb Campbell/Shutterstock; 4, © National Park Service; 5, © Joshlaymons/ Wikipedia Creative Commons; 7, © James Urbach/Superstock; 8T, © William Leaman/Alamy; 8B, © Tim Zurowski/All Canada Photos/Alamy; 9, © Pacific Northwest Photo/Shutterstock; 10T, © Evgeniy Ayupov/Shutterstock; 10C, © Pan Xunbin/ Shutterstock; 10B, © hwongcc/Shutterstock; 11, © Joe McDonald/Visuals Unlimited/Science Photo Library; 12, © Gordon E. Robertson; 13, © Illini Images by Steve Patterson; 14, © Gregory Synstelien/Shutterstock; 15, © Jack Thomas/Alamy; 16, © McDonald Wildlife Photography/Animals Animals; 17, 18, 19, © James Urbach/Superstock; 20 © Bird Images/Istockphoto; 21, © lightstalker/iStockphoto; 22, © Rick Wylie/Shutterstock, © Colin D. Young/Shutterstock, © Gerald A. DeBoer/Shutterstock, and © S. Charlie Brown/FLPA; 23TL, © Deb Campbell/Shutterstock; 23TC, © B. Calkins/Shutterstock; 23TR, © Anneka/ Shutterstock; 23BL, © Andrey Pavlov/Shutterstock; 23BC, © James Urbach/Superstock; 23BR, © lightstalker/iStockphoto.

Publisher: Kenn Goin
Creative Director: Spencer Brinker
Design: Emma Randall
Editor: Mark J. Sachner
Photo Researcher: Ruby Tuesday Books Ltd

Library of Congress Cataloging-in-Publication Data

Phillips, Dee, 1967–
    Woodpecker / by Dee Phillips.
        p. cm. — (Treed: animal life in the trees)
    Includes bibliographical references and index.
    ISBN-13: 978-1-61772-913-3 (library binding)
    ISBN-10: 1-61772-913-2 (library binding)
    1. Woodpeckers—Juvenile literature. I. Title.
    QL696.P56P46 2014
    598.7'2—dc23

                              2013011525

For more information, write to Bearport Publishing Company, Inc., 45 West 21st Street, Suite 3B, New York, New York 10010. Printed in the United States of America.

10 9 8 7 6 5 4 3 2 1

Contents

Strange Sounds

Deep in a forest, a bird is making a strange drumming noise.

It's a woodpecker, and he's striking a tree trunk with his beak.

This noise tells his partner that he is ready to **mate**.

Spring has arrived, and it's time for woodpeckers to have chicks.

Woodpeckers live, find their food, and raise their babies in trees.

woodpecker

forest

woodpecker

Imagine someone you know has never seen a woodpecker. Describe what the bird looks like to that person.

All About Woodpeckers

There are 250 different kinds of woodpeckers.

These birds live in forests around the world.

One kind of woodpecker that lives in North America is the pileated (PYE-lee-AY-tuhd) woodpecker.

Some pileated woodpeckers make their homes in **evergreen** forests.

Others live in forests where the trees lose their leaves in the fall.

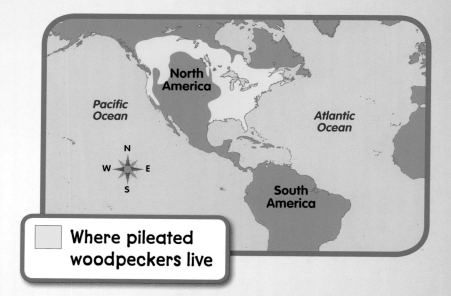

North America

Pacific Ocean

Atlantic Ocean

N

W   E

S

South America

Where pileated woodpeckers live

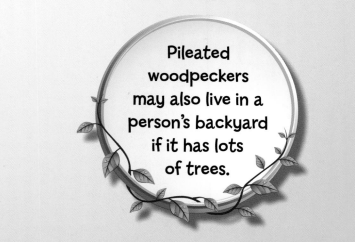

Pileated woodpeckers may also live in a person's backyard if it has lots of trees.

pileated woodpecker

How do you think woodpeckers got their name?

Meet a Woodpecker

A pileated woodpecker is a large bird with black-and-white feathers.

It has a **crest** of red feathers on its head.

Like all woodpeckers, it has a long, sharp beak.

Its beak is strong enough to peck holes in wood!

male

crest

female

crest

The heads of male and female woodpeckers are different in two ways. What are the differences?
(The answer to this question is on page 24.)

beak

From the tip of its beak to the tip of its tail feathers, an adult pileated woodpecker is about 19 inches (48 cm) long.

tail feathers

Pecking for Insects

Woodpeckers eat **insects** that live inside trees.

To find food, the birds peck holes in tree trunks.

The loud, hard pecking makes a drumming sound.

After finding an insect, a woodpecker grabs its meal with its long tongue.

Woodpeckers don't only make holes in trees to find food. Why else might woodpeckers peck holes in tree trunks?

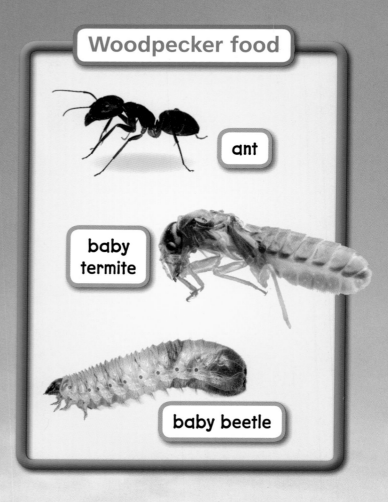

Woodpecker food

ant

baby termite

baby beetle

tongue

A woodpecker uses its long tongue to grab insects from inside a tree.

Building a Nest Hole

When spring arrives, it's time for male and female woodpeckers to raise a family.

First, the male woodpecker pecks a hole in a large tree.

Once the hole is big enough, he climbs inside.

Then he continues pecking until he has made a small room.

The room will be the birds' nest.

male woodpecker pecking a nest hole

It takes three to six weeks for woodpeckers to build their nest hole. The male does most of the work, but the female helps, too.

nest hole

wood chip from inside the nest

13

Woodpecker Eggs

Once the nest hole is finished, the woodpeckers mate.

A few days later, the female lays three to five eggs in the nest.

The parents take turns sitting on the eggs to keep them warm.

The chicks inside the eggs need warmth to grow.

finished nest hole

male woodpecker

Lots of small wood chips that the birds pecked from inside the tree lie on the floor of the nest hole. These wood chips make a soft bed for the eggs.

wood chips

eggs in nest hole

15

Busy Parents

After 18 days, the woodpecker chicks **hatch** from the eggs.

The baby birds' eyes are closed, and the chicks' bodies have no feathers.

By the time the chicks are 15 days old, their eyes have opened.

Some of their black, white, and red feathers have grown in, too.

15-day-old chicks

Woodpecker parents spend most of their time finding food for their hungry chicks. They peck for insects and then feed them to their babies.

parent woodpecker feeding a chick

Growing Chicks

At 20 days old, the big chicks peek out of the nest hole.

When their parents arrive with food, the chicks squawk.

At 28 days old, the chicks are ready to leave the nest.

They jump out of the nest hole and fly from tree to tree with their parents.

20-day-old chicks

Each woodpecker pair has its own area, or **territory**, in a forest. The woodpeckers make loud drumming sounds with their beaks to tell other woodpeckers to stay out of their territory.

All Grown Up

Woodpecker chicks stay with their parents all summer.

The adults teach their chicks how to peck at trees to find insects.

Then, in the fall, each young woodpecker goes off to live on its own.

By spring, the woodpeckers will be adults and ready to find partners.

Then it will be time for them to make nests and raise families of their own!

parent woodpecker

two-month-old chick

Pileated woodpeckers can live for more than 12 years.

adult woodpecker

Science Lab

A Tree Hole Home

A hole in a tree is a dry safe place for an animal to have its babies.

Like woodpeckers, the animals pictured below use tree holes as nests or dens.

Choose one of the animals below and then use the Internet and books to research how it lives.

Next, make a chart like the one shown to compare and contrast the life of a woodpecker with the animal you've chosen.

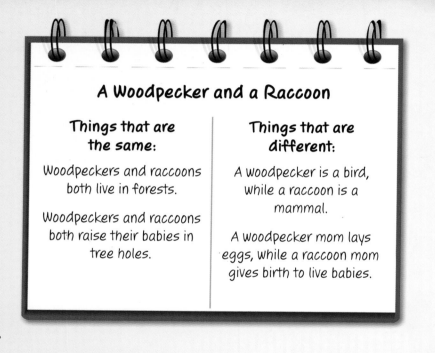

A Woodpecker and a Raccoon

Things that are the same:	Things that are different:
Woodpeckers and raccoons both live in forests.	A woodpecker is a bird, while a raccoon is a mammal.
Woodpeckers and raccoons both raise their babies in tree holes.	A woodpecker mom lays eggs, while a raccoon mom gives birth to live babies.

gray squirrel   macaw parrot   raccoon   barn owl

Science Words

crest (KREST) a ridge or tuft of feathers on a bird's head

evergreen (EV-ur-*green*) a tree or other plant that has green leaves or needles all year round

hatch (HACH) to break out of an egg

insects (IN-sekts) small animals that have six legs, three main body parts, two antennae, and a hard covering called an exoskeleton

mate (MAYT) to come together in order to have young

territory (TEHR-uh-tor-ee) the area where an animal lives and finds its food

Index

Read More

Gray, Susan Heinrichs. *The Life Cycle of Birds (Life Cycles)*. Chicago: Heinemann (2012).

Lawrence, Ellen. *A Bird's Life (Animal Diaries: Life Cycles)*. New York: Bearport (2013).

Schuetz, Kari. *Woodpeckers (Blastoff! Readers: Backyard Wildlife)*. Minneapolis: Bellwether Media (2012).

Learn More Online

To learn more about woodpeckers, visit **www.bearportpublishing.com/Treed**

About the Author

Dee Phillips lives near the ocean on the southwest coast of England. She develops and writes nonfiction and fiction books for children of all ages. Dee's biggest ambition is to one day walk the entire coastline of Britain—it will take about ten months!

Answer for Page 8

A male woodpecker has a red patch on each cheek, and his red crest spreads from the top of his head down to his beak.